AF411546

JUDI WERTHEIN & LEANDRO ERLICH

TURISMO

LA HABANA, CUBA

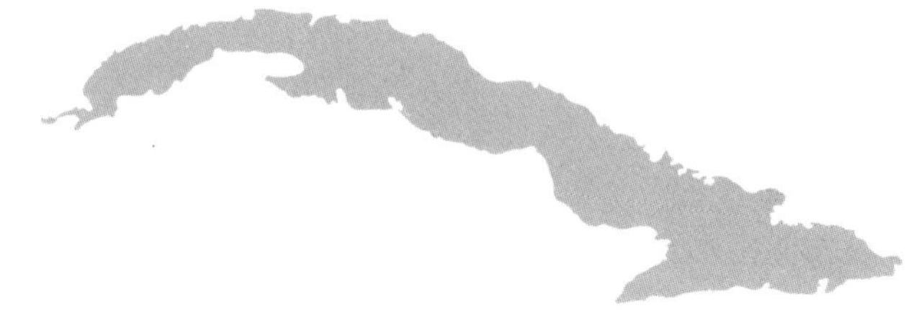

KENT

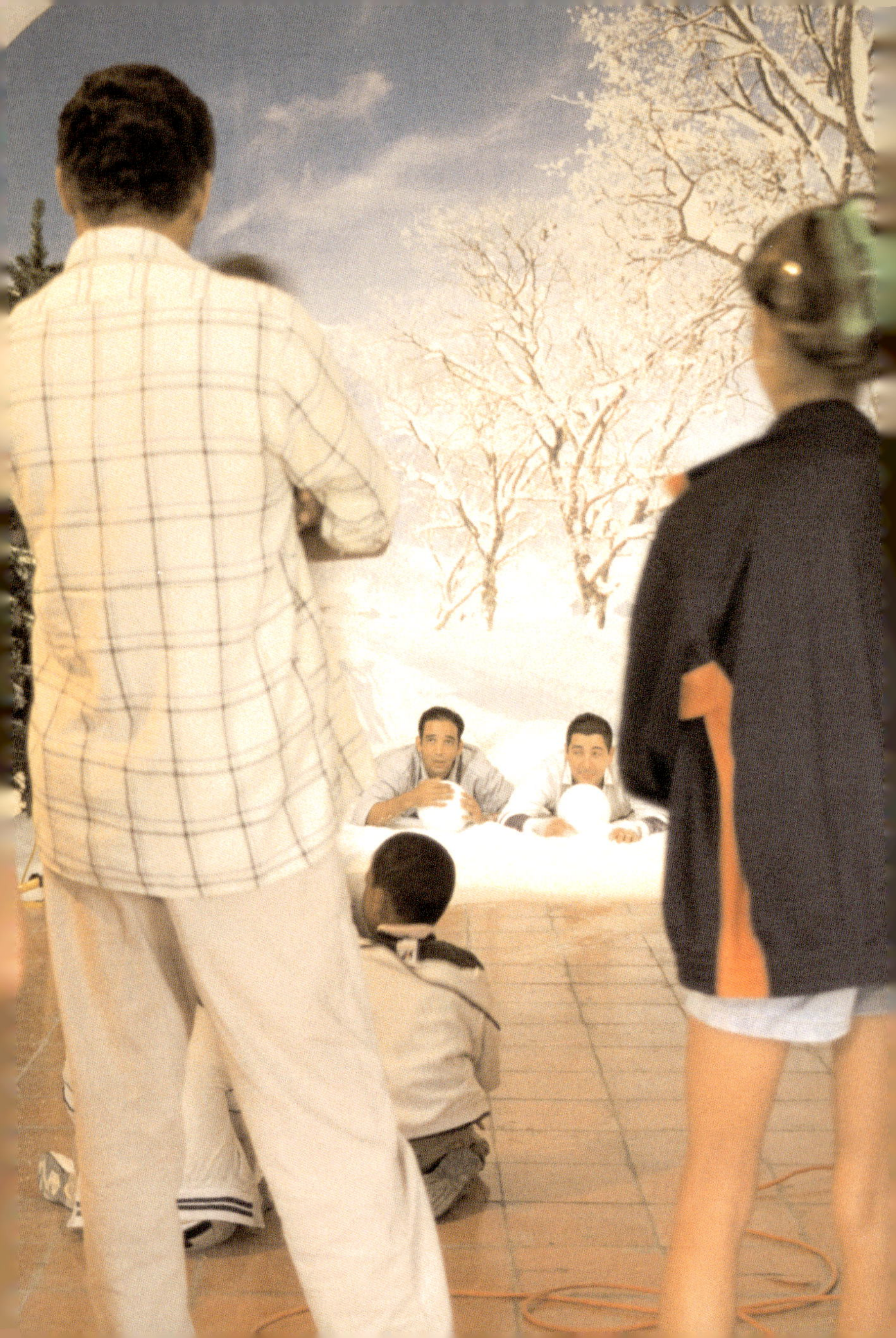

The Project

We flew to Cuba from New York via Jamaica with twelve outsize crates, two suitcases, and 6000 sheets of Polaroid film. We were traveling to take part in Havana's Seventh Biennial, the theme of which would be "Communication in Difficult Times: One Closer to the Other".

On the basis of this point of view, we began to think about the possibilities, given the fact that our collaborations have always resulted in site-specific works that would be meaningful in and for one particular place.

For Cuba, we wished to compose an idea that would allow us to come into close contact with the Cubans. A project connected with the reality of Cuba, which would result in an actual meeting with the public, rather than the mere manifestation of an artist that was alien to their context. We would transport the meeting place in the form of a landscape, a fantasized imaginary situation.

We encouraged the participation of the public, creating the experience of their being tourists. Tourism is a global industry that encourages communication between different countries through traveling as a form of recreation.

For Cuba today, Tourism represents a highly complex factor within society. It is tourists who reach Cuba to spend their vacations, a most important source of income and foreign currency for the country. Simultaneously, this industry eventually creates a great contradiction within the country's social and political structure.

We were aware of the reality of life in Cuba, and from the very beginning we were also aware of the fact that a political meaning could be ascribed to any proposal in Havana. It was important for us to generate an opportunity within Cuban reality in which we could underline the everyday reality of the people without creating a political manifesto.

Our installation was assigned to "La Cabaña", a historical fortress dating back to the colonial period and which in later times was used for other purposes, such as the residence of Fulgencio Batista, a jail, and, after the 1959 revolution, the headquarters of the Comandancia, led by the Che Guevara. Today this Comandancia building, the yellow house, located right opposite our exhibition hall, houses the Museum of the Che, while the Fortress of "La Cabaña", where there are government offices and a military regiment is still in charge of the cannon ceremony (1), forms part of the tourist circuit of Havana.

When we finished setting up the installation, and even before that, the people strolling around "La Cabaña" approached us with great enthusiasm. Everybody wanted to take part in the project, as cheerful as we had been while thinking up our project. Some people even brought us gifts, poems and cigars.

Yanet, a beautiful young brunette, was the assistant assigned by the Biennial to collaborate with us in the exhibition hall. She helped us organize the public so that everybody could pose in the set while they were being photo-transported to the Alps.

One of the first, and very agreeable echoes of our work came from the office next door. There, some people were joking with their colleagues about a trip to Switzerland and showing the Polaroid prints to prove it.

On the third day a young man brought along a sweater, so that the photo would look more realistic and convincing. The people that came in after he did kept borrowing his sweater for their own pictures. Some days later a beautiful girl came to the set wearing a splendid colonial dress (the type of dress that includes a hoop skirt, a fan and a back comb, worn by girls in celebration of their 15th birthday). The man in charge of the garbage in "La Cabaña" approached the place with his green cart; and even Marisabel Salinas, who drives a tourist-laden coach in "La Fortaleza", showed up with her horse and gave a Caribbean touch to the Alpine landscape.

The soldiers of the regiment in "La Cabaña" always formed part of the public. On one of the first days, a lieutenant approached us, and after having the soldiers left the hall, he unsmilingly asked us not to take photos of the soldiers in their uniforms. We explained to him that this was an artistic project and in no way meant to create trouble. The lieutenant refused to listen to us and again asked us not to take photos of the soldiers in service. We showed him photos we had taken the day before in order to illustrate the idea of the project, and in one of them he recognized a high ranking officer smiling and posing on the skis. Upon seeing this, the lieutenant asked whether we charged for the photos and we answered that all the participants were entitled to take their photos for free. Next, he asked if we would take his photo, posing with his daughters.

Tourism became quite an event in itself on account of the variegated public summoned by the Biennial. Besides the general public, there were personalities of the world of art, curators and critics, all of them mingled in the adventure.

We hope that the selection of images in this small book convey all the humor, the spontaneous joy and the wonders in this encounter.

Due to the situation derived from the embargo imposed by the United States —and in order to avoid trouble for their tourists— Cuban immigration officers never stamp passports. As we had only been in Jamaica in transit, we returned to New York twenty days later after officially having spent all that time "nowhere in the world". This was in part true since we had created a space where the fiction we had built up opened like a parenthesis and transported us to a land of fantasy, full of Caribbean joy, a mixture of snow and heat.

We are deeply indebted to the organizers of the Biennial for their invitation. To Kent Gallery, to the Ministry of Foreign Affairs of Argentina, to the Polaroid Foundation, and to the Pan-American Cultural Exchange for their extraordinary support, and very special thanks to all those who accompanied us through these impossible vacations in the Caribbean Alps.

To the beautiful people of Cuba, our gratitude.
Leandro Erlich & Judi Werthein (Translated by Myriam Schlossberg)

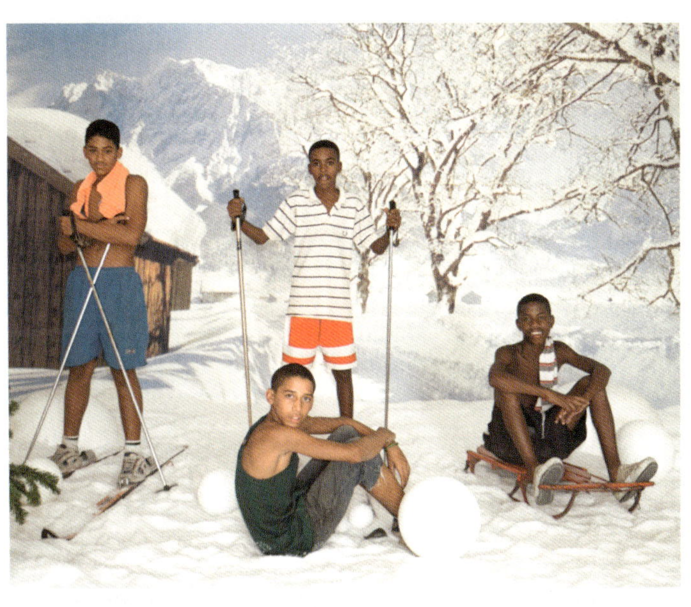

Reynaldo, Dagmar, Andy y Yandri

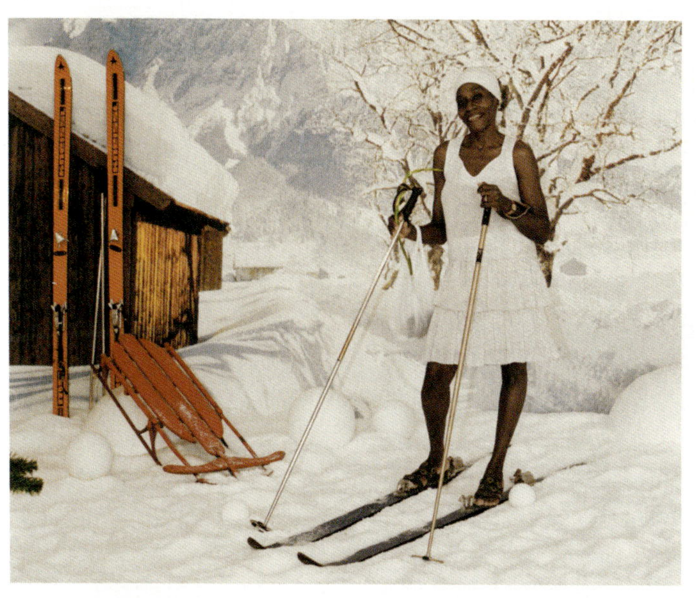

Magdalena

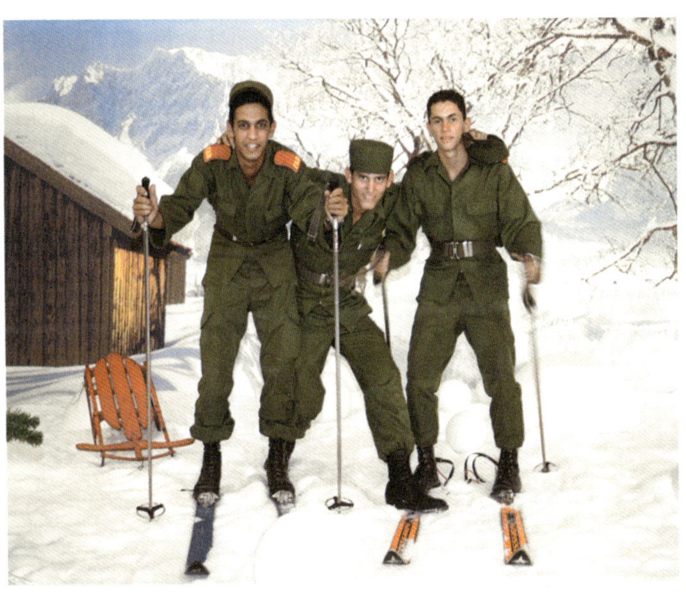

Soldados Sergio, Jesus y Fleitas

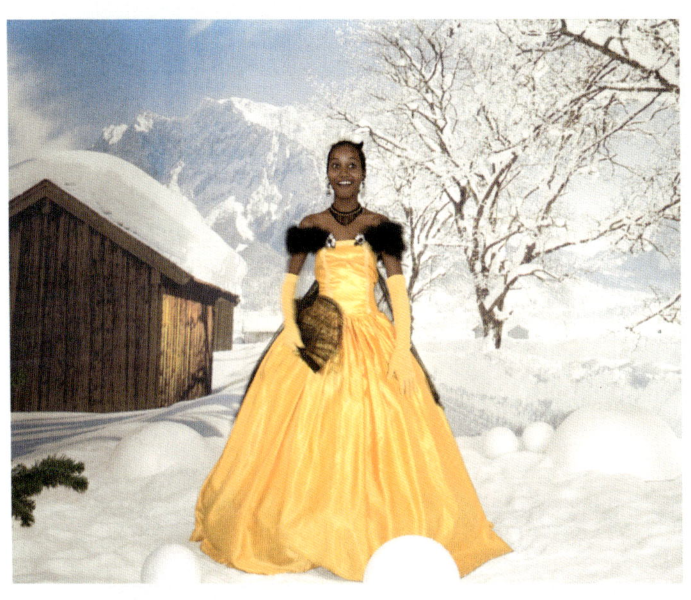

Ailin

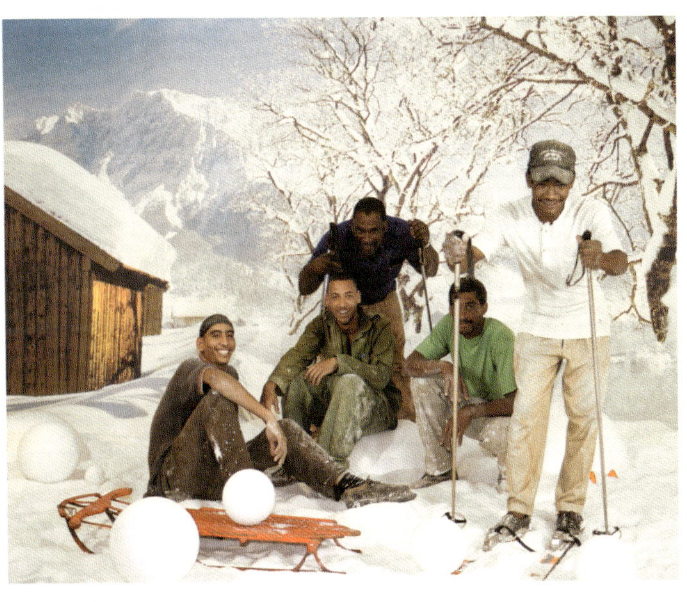

Alain , Yasdil, Floro, Ariel y Pablo

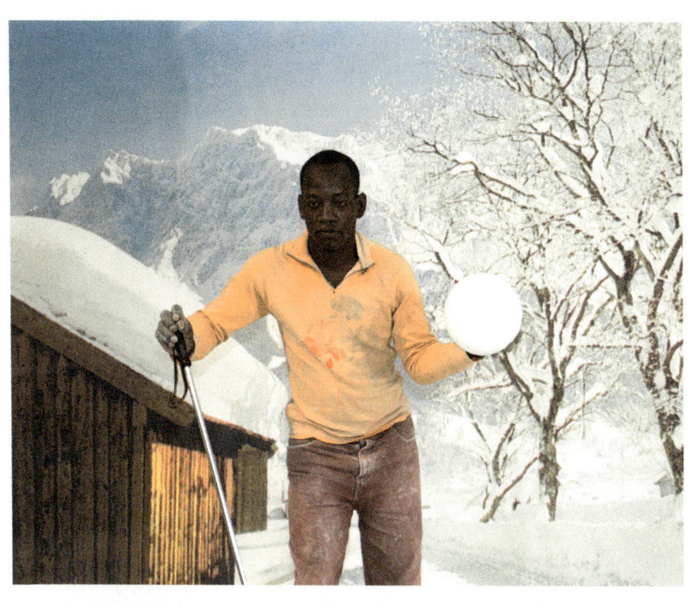

Raidel

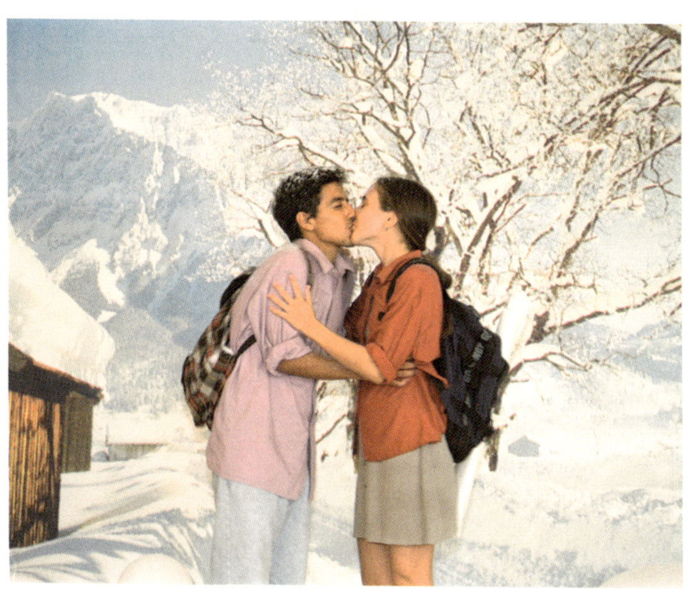

Irving y Maria

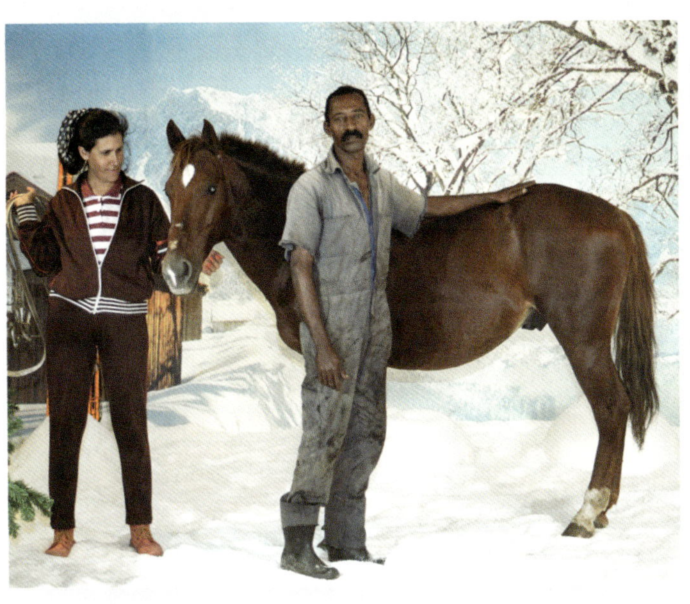

Marisbel, her horse and her spouse

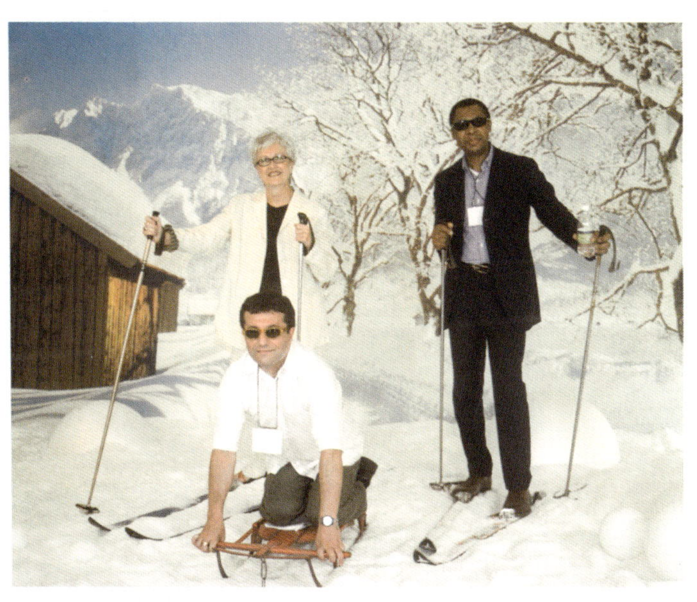

Curators

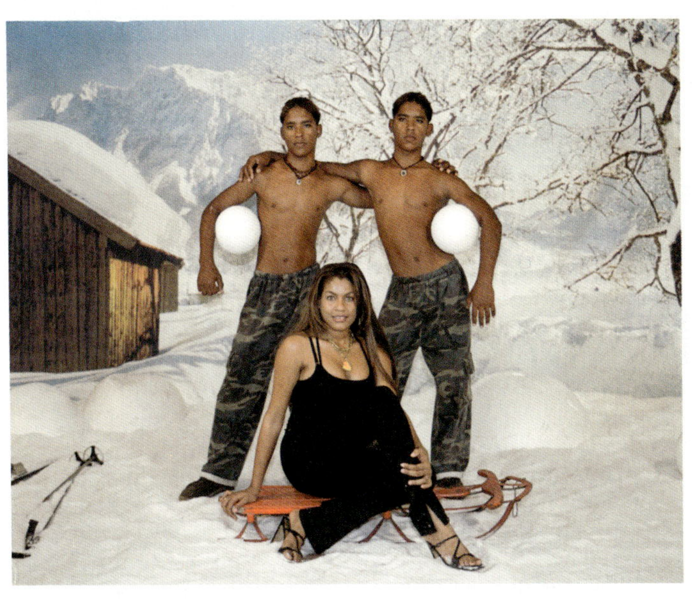

Yaima, Denier y Rainier

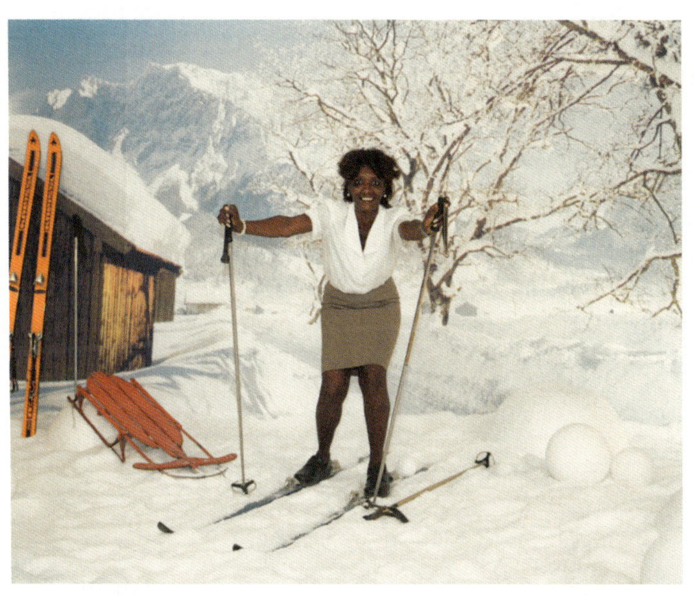

Soraida

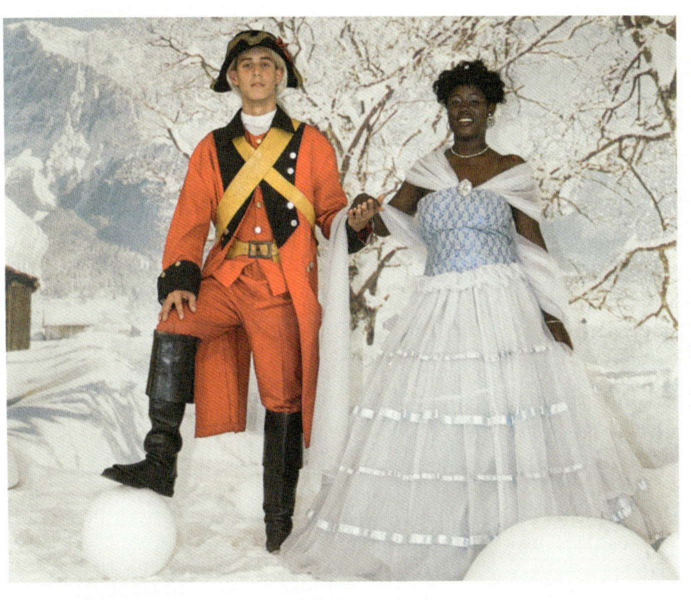

Soldados y Quinceñera

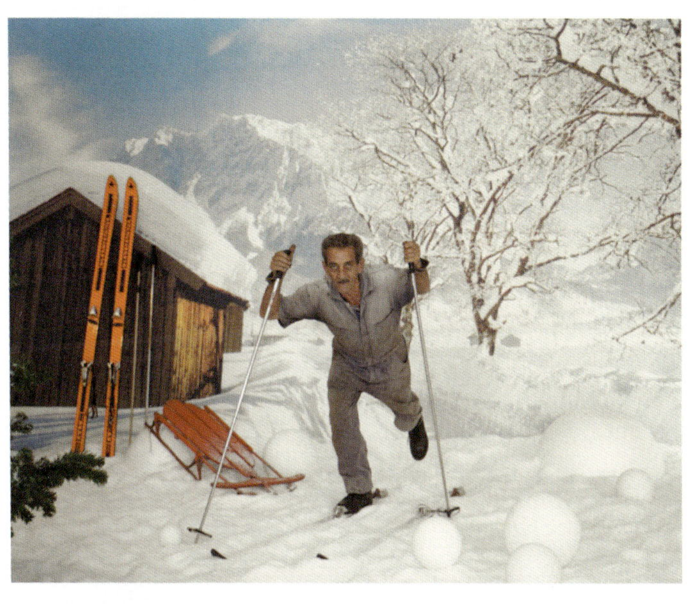

José

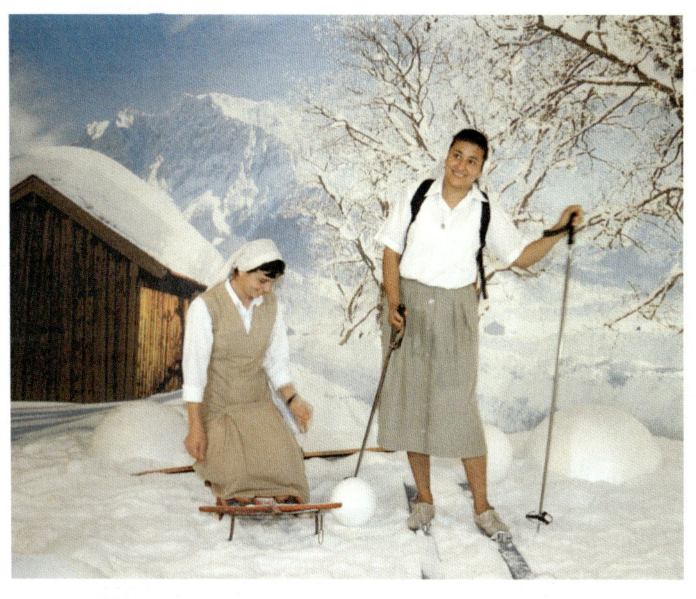

Nuns

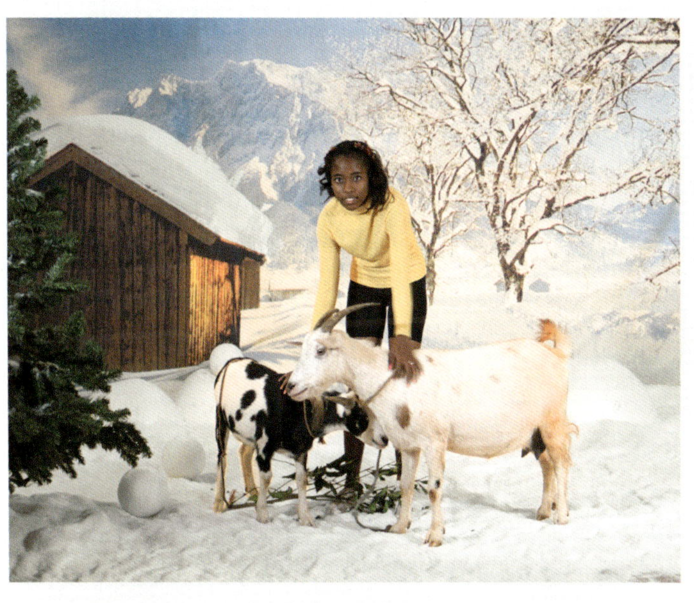

Edilia and her goats

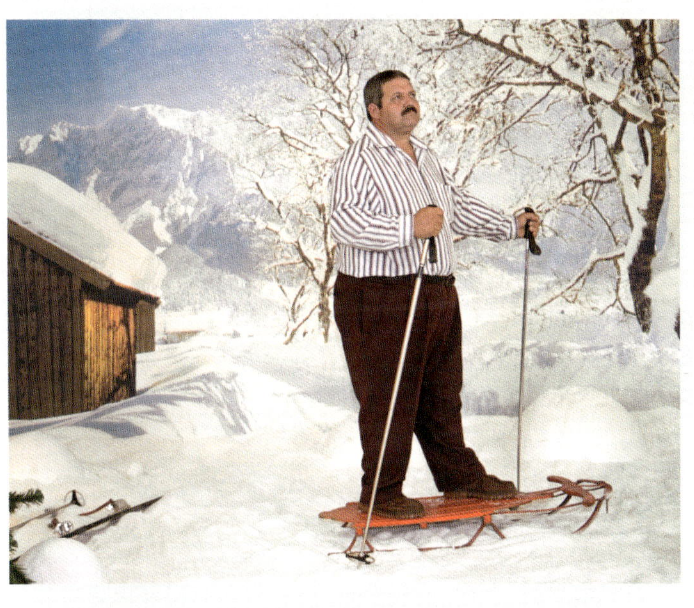

Ernesto

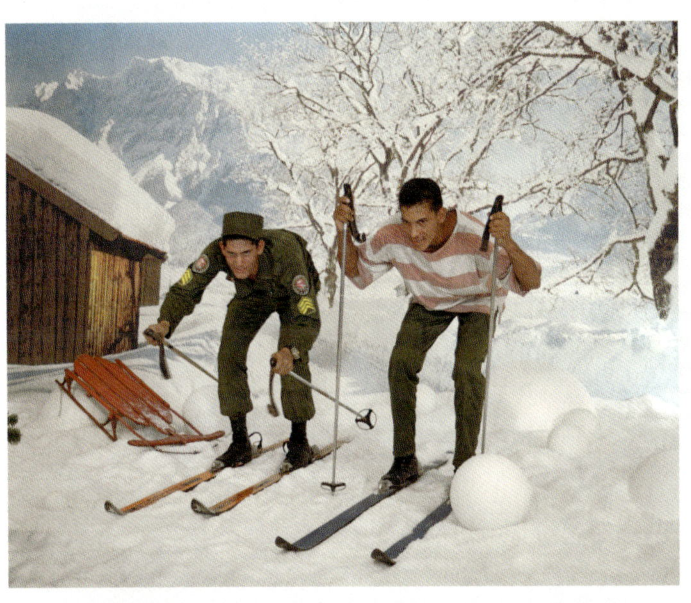

Soldados Michael y Yordis

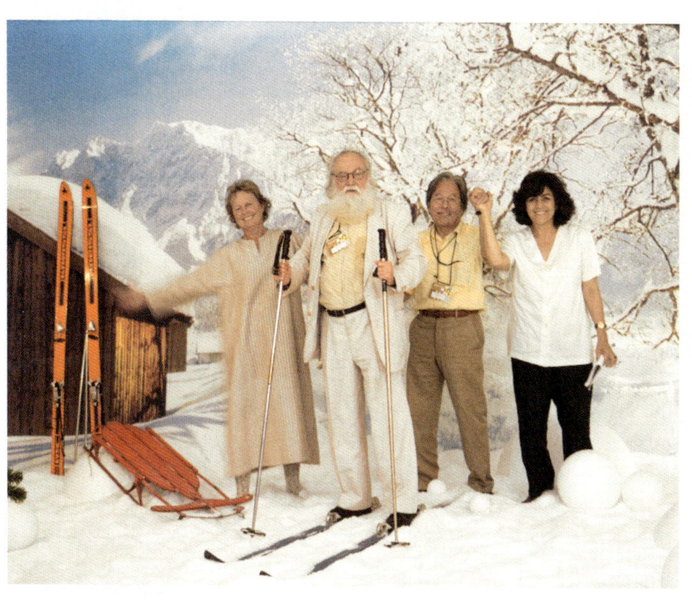

The Jury

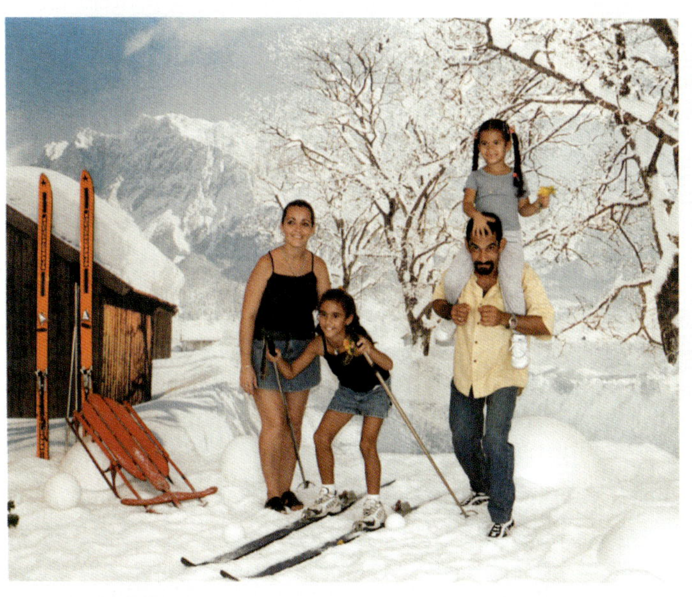

Familia Ramos

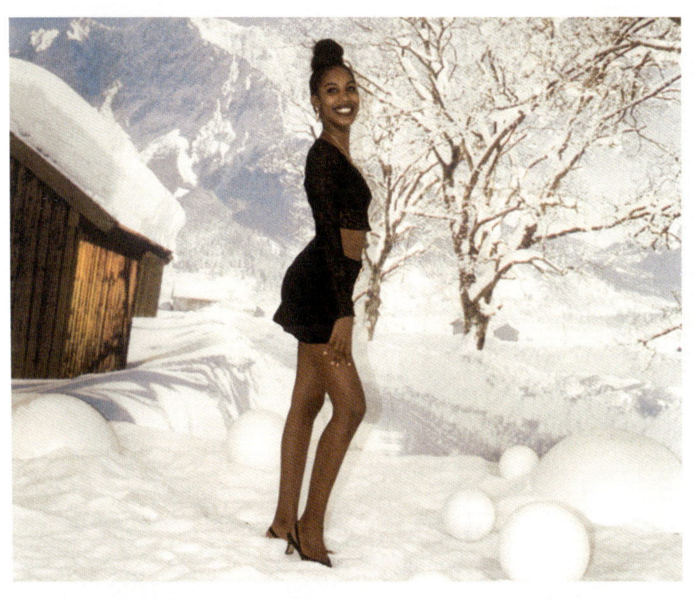

Dana

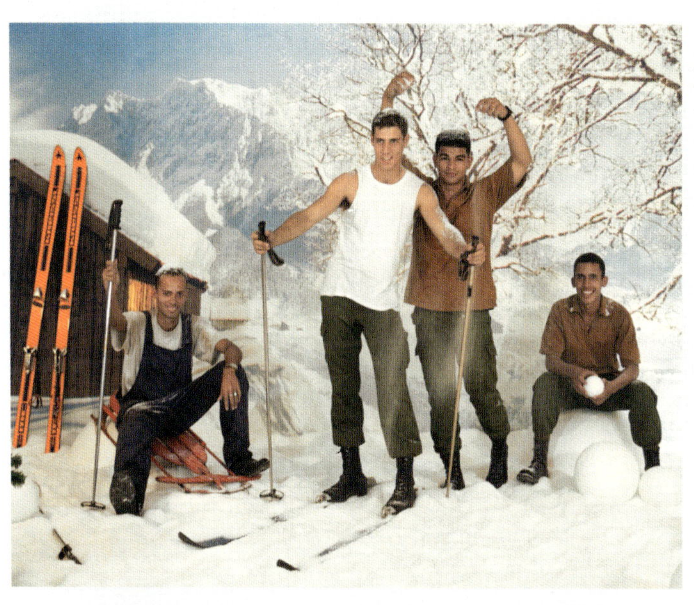

Daniel, Alexander, Yariel y Osman

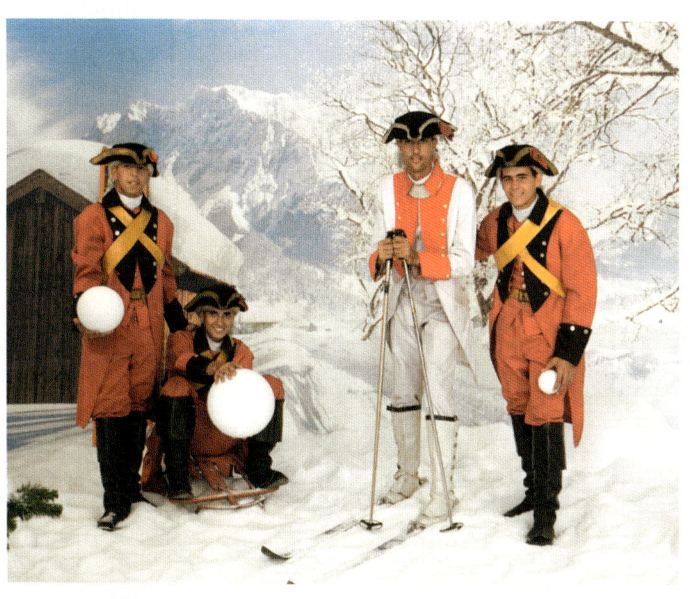

Soldados dressed for the Cannon Cermony

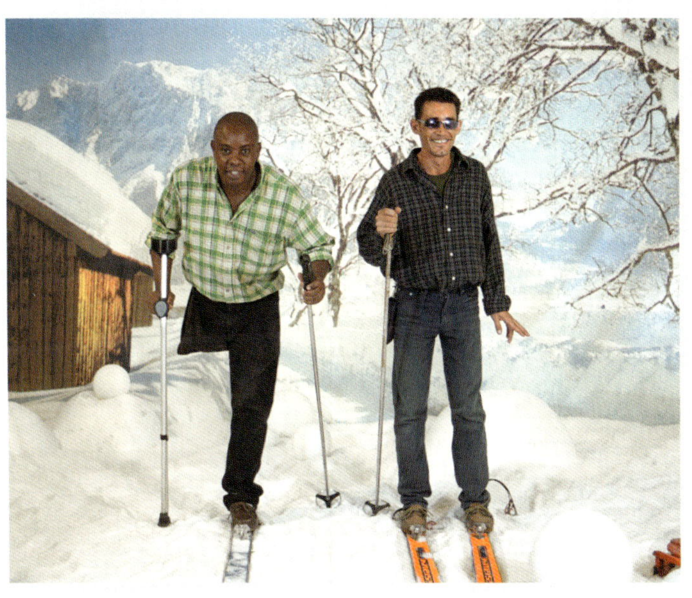

Rene y Carlos

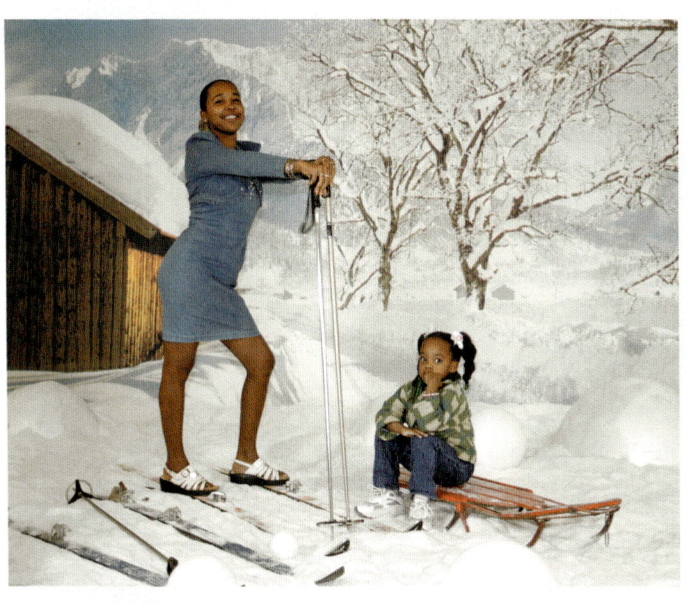

Grisel and her daughter Jessica

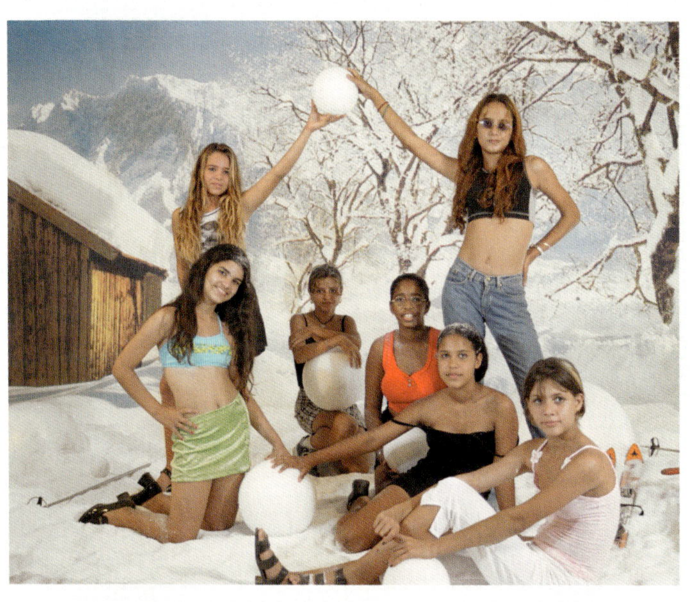

Rebeca, Yanisley, Heidi , Yaneisi, Yanelis, Yusmari y Juliet

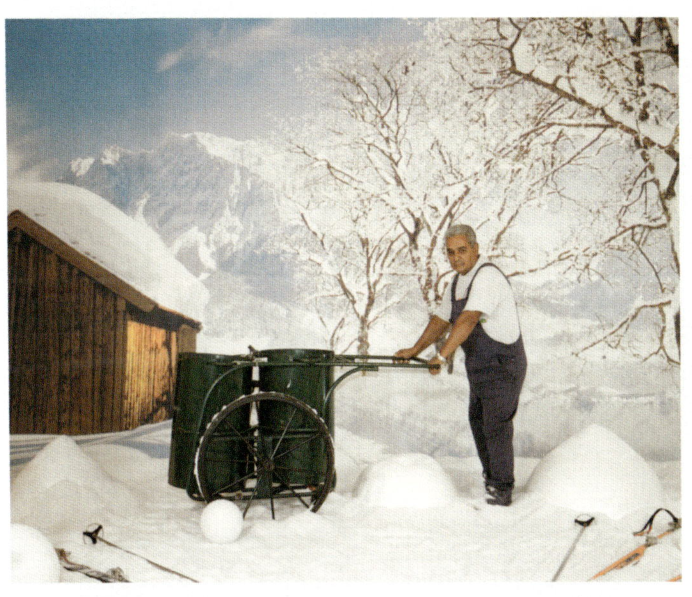

Benancio

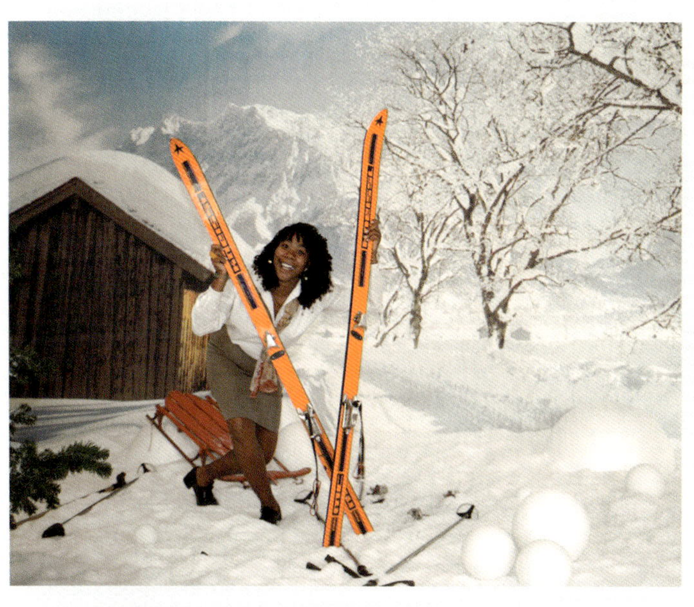

Inoris

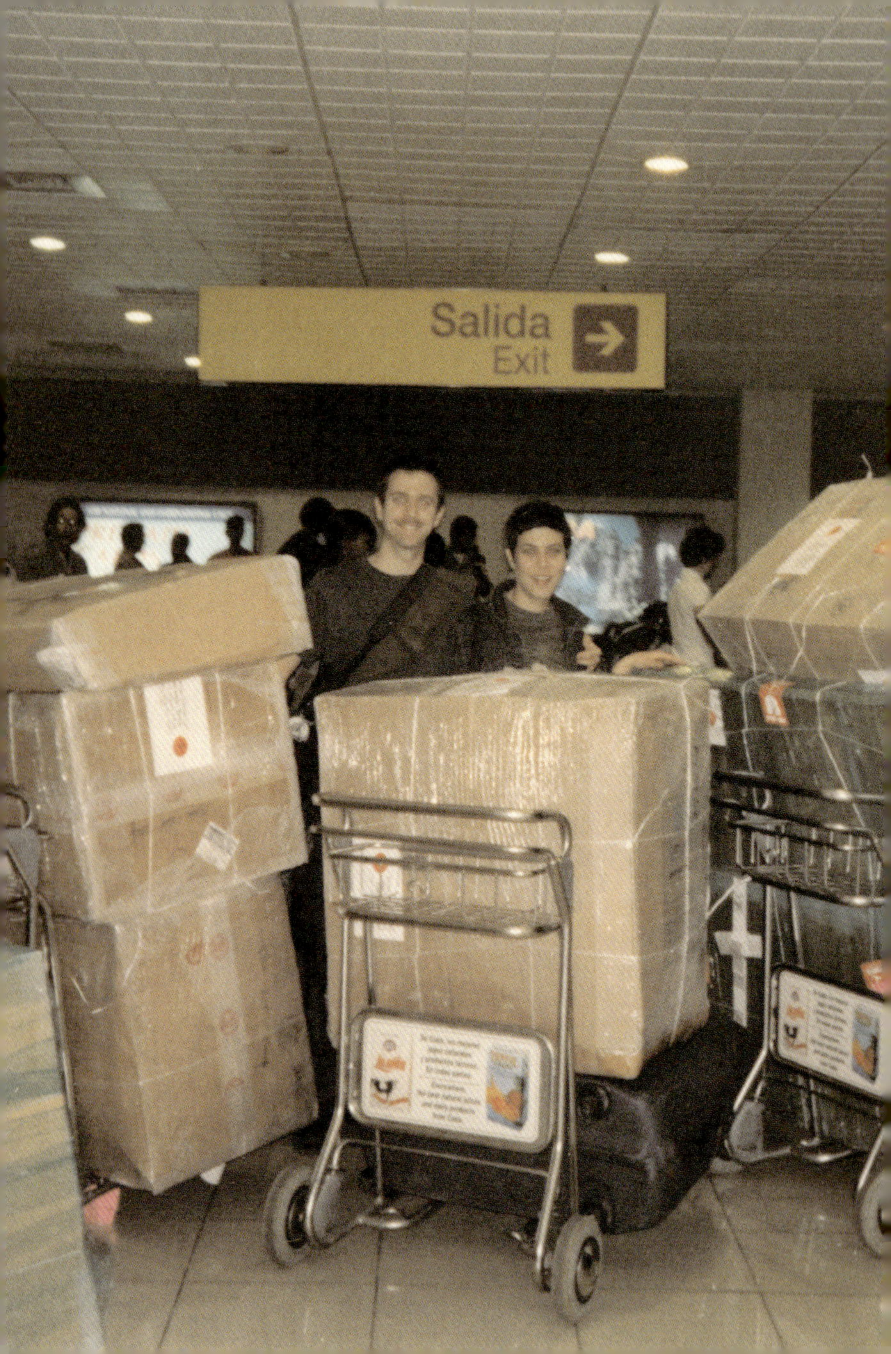

Salida
Exit

Leandro Erlich

SOLO EXHIBITIONS
2001   *NEIGHBORS: an installation by Leandro Erlich*   El Museo del Barrio, New York, NY
        TOURISM (collaboration with Judi Werthein) Kent Gallery, New York, NY
2000   *6 feet under(collaboration with Judi Werthein)* White Box Gallery, New York, NY
        Ruth Benzacar Gallery   Buenos Aires, Argentina
1999   *El Living*   Kent Gallery   New York, NY
        Rain Moody Gallery Houston, TX
1997   *Inner City* General Consulate of Argentina, New York, NY
1993   Centro Cultural Recoleta   Buenos Aires
        Espacio Giesso   Buenos Aires
1991   Centro Cultural Recoleta   Buenos Aires

SELECTED GROUP EXHIBITIONS
2001   *Leandro Erlich: The Swimming Pool* 49th Venice Biennale (Argentina)
        Fondaco dei Tedeschi via Rialto, Venice, Italy
        VOX 2001 Kent Gallery, New York, NY
2000   *TOURISM (collaboration with Judi Werthein)* VII Bienal de La Habana, Cuba
        Whitney Biennal. Whitney Museum of American Art, New York, NY (catalogue)
        Natural Deceits: Ten Texas Artists. Modern Art Museum, Fort Worth, TX
1999   *Core 1999.* Museum of Fine Arts, Houston, TX (catalogue).
        Paralelos / Paralelas. Fondo Nacional des las Artes, ARCO Madrid, Spain (catalogue).
1998   *Core 1998.* Museum of Fine Arts, Houston, TX (catalogue).
1997   *First Mercosur Biennial Art Show* Porto Alegre, Brazil
1996   AEIUO Installations   Centro Cultural Recoleta, Buenos Aires
1995   *Twelve Argentinian Artists* United Nations, Buenos Aires
        Taller De Barracas Ruth Benzacar Gallery, Buenos Aires
        Spring Roll (collaboration with Judith Werthein) Peru Square, Buenos Aires

SELECTED AWARDS
2000   Premio Leonardo Museo Nacional de Bellas Artes, Buenos Aires
1998   Eliza Prize, Core Program, Museum of Fine Arts, Houston
1997   Core Program Houston, Pan-American Cultural Exchange-Fundacion Antorchal
1995   Mention of Honor Braque Prize of Objects, French Embassy, Buenos Aires
1994   Taller de Barracas Core Fellowship, Fundacion Antorchas, Buenos Aires
1992   Fondo Nacional de las Artes, Buenos Aires

BIBLIOGRAPHY

Argentino usa voyeurismo na arte Correio Do Povo. (Brazil). 10 October 1997 p. 20
VII Bienal de La Habana Centro de Arte Contemporaneo Wilfredo Lam, Consejo Nacional de Artes Plasticas, Cuba 2000 (catalogue)
Como el Obselisco del centro , pero en la Boca y de hierro, La Razon 12 December 1994 p 15
Goings on About Town: Leandro Erlich The New Yorker 11 October 1999 p. 23
Talent Pool: Leandro Erlich (color section cover) Houston Chronicle 21 March 1999
Arenes, Carolina *En Buenos Aires habría un Nuevo obelisco* La Nacion 18 February 1995
Battistozzi, Ana Maria *Una vasta telaraña de espejismos* Clarin 30 September 2000
Cantor, Judi *In the Art of the City* Miami New Times 1 April 2001
Cash, Stephanie *Leandro Erlich at Kent* Art in America December 1999
Cotter, Holland *Leandro Erlich at El Museo del Barrio* New York Times 17 April 2001
Erlich, Leandro *Un obelisco en La Boca* La Prensa 1995
Fernandez, Jorge Luis *Un mundo de ilusiones* La Nacion 26 September 2000
Grinstein, Eva *Havana Biennial* Flash Art March-April, 2001
Herzberg, Julia P. *NEIGHBORS: an installation by Leandro Erlich* El Museo del Barrio, New York 2001
Israel, Nico *VII Bienal de La Habana* Artforum February 2001 p. 147-148
Johnson, Ken. *Leandro Erlich: El Living* New York Times 8 October 1999 p. E37
Johnson, Patricia. *Exprit de Core* Houston Chronicle 21 March 1999 p. 8 - 9
Katzentstein, Ines *Erlich: the eye witness* Argentine Consulate, New York 1997 (catalogue)
Kimmelman, Michael *A new team at the Whitney makes its Biennial Pitch* New York Times 24 March 2000
Lebenglik, Fabian *El gabinete del Dr. Benedit: Bairon, di Girolamo, El Azem y Erlich* Pagina 12 April 1999 p. 26
Lebenglik, Fabian *Verdad, Mentira y Ficion* Pagina 12 3 October 2000
Levin, Kim *Voice Choices: Leandro Erlich* Village Voice 14 September 1999 p. 82
Levin, Kim *Leandro Erlich's Disappearing Act: PARALLEL UNIVERSE* Village Voice Feb 2001
MacAdam, Barbara A. *Leandro Erlich* Artnews October 1999 p. 188 illus. in color
Maio, Hugo & Marita Hermo *Proyecto: Obelisco en la Boca* Publicacion Mensual Rumbos February 1995
Navarro, Santiago Garcia *Pensar el espacio* La Nacion 16 April 1999
Noorthoorn, Victoria *Warning: Perception Requires Involvement* White Box Gallery, New York 2000
Relyea, Lane *The Ins and Outs of this Year's Core Show* Core 1998 (catalogue) illustrated
Rizzo, Patricia *Leandro Erlich* ARCO '99 Madrid: Fondo Nacional de Las Artes (catalogue) pp. 91 - 99
Sanchez, Julio *Un artista usa plastico planea construir un obelisco de hierro en La Boca* La Maga 1995
Stein Greben, Deirdre *Strolling Under the Swimming Pool* Artnews June 2000 p.128-129
Stetler, Pepper *Through the Looking Glass: the Art of Leandro Erlich* Museo Spring 2000
Szatmary, Peter *Essay in Reach* Core 1999 (catalogue)
Torresi, Leonardo *El obelisco mellizo* Clarin 15 January 1995 p 8
Verlichak, Victoria *Percepciones alteradas* Revista Noticias 7 October 2000
Viveros-Faune, Christian *Whitney Biennial Artists* New York Press 4 April 2000
Vogel, Carol *Choosing a Palette of Biennial Artists* New York Times 8 December 1999 p. E5
Whitney Museum of American Art Whitney Biennial 2000 Bulletin January 2000 p.102-103
Whitney Museum of American Art Whitney Biennial 2000 (catalogue) p. 102 & 103 April 2000

Judi Werthein

SOLO EXHIBITIONS

2001	*Tourism (in collaboration with Leandro Erlich)* Kent Gallery, New York
2000	*Skin* Museo de Arte Contemporaneo, Bahia Blanca, Argentina
	Ruth Benzacar Galeria de Arte, Buenos Aires, Argentina
	Skin II Centro Cultural de San Martin, Buenos Aires, Argentina
	6 feet under(collaboration with Leandro Erlich) White Box Gallery, New York, NY
1997	*Judi Werthein: Paintings.* General Consulate of Argentina, New York
1996	*Jorge Ruiz vs. Julio Cesar Ramirez.* Mun Galeria, Buenos Aires, Argentina
1995	*Spring Roll (in collaboration with Leandro Erlich)* Peru Square, Buenos Aires,
1991	*Cemento* Espacio Arte, Buenos Aires, Argentina

SELECTED GROUP EXHIBITIONS

2001	*Autorretrato* Centro Cultural Borges, Buenos Aires, Argentina
	VOX 2001 Kent Gallery, New York, NY
2000	*Artists in the Marketplace.* Bronx Museum of Art, New York, NY
	Tourism (in collaboration with Leandro Erlich) VII Bienal de La Habana, Cuba
	Pet Show Curated by Tim Tyzel Cynthia Broan Gallery, New York, NY
	25 Anniversary Moody Gallery, Houston, TX
	Summer Selections Moody Gallery, Houston, TX
1998	*The Art of Memory* Center for Curatorial Studies Museum, Bard College, Annadale-on-Hudson, NY
1997	*Sassy Nuggets* Andrew Kreps Gallery New York, NY
1996	*Premios Austria* National Museum of Fine Arts, Buenos Aires, Argentina
1995	*Bienal Chandon* National Museum of Fine Arts, Buenos Aires, Argentina
	Premios Mayorazgo National Museum of Fine Arts, Buenos Aires, Argentina

BIBLIOGRAPHY

Arte contemporaneo y de calidad, Dos muestras de Judi Werthein <u>Revista</u> June, 1996

Artists in the Marketplace Bronx Museum for the Arts, NY (catalogue) October 2000

<u>*VII Bienal de La Habana*</u> Centro de Arte Contemporaneo Wilfredo Lam, Consejo Nacional de Artes Plasticas, Cuba (catalogue) 2000

<u>*Bienal Chandon*</u> Museo Nacional de Bellas Artes, Buenos Aires (catalogue) 1995

<u>*Premios Austria 1996*</u> National Museum of Fine Arts, Buenos Aires (catalogue) 1995

<u>*Premios Mayorazgo*</u> National Museum of Fine Arts, Buenos Aires (catalogue) 1995

Abadi, Corinne Sacca *El Agua Immovil* <u>Revista</u> 3 puntos 15 June 2000

Artusi, Maria Cecilia *No al Arte* <u>La Nación</u> October 1995

Bosco, Marcelo *Judi Werthein al otro Lado de la Realidad* <u>El Arca</u> No. 21 June 1996

Bosco, Marcelo *Jorge Ruiz vs. Cesar Ramirez* Mun Galeria de Arte, Buenos Aires (catalogue) May 1996

Cantor, Judi *In the Art of the City* <u>Miami New Times</u> 1 April 2001

Cotter, Holland *Sassy Nuggets* <u>The New York Times</u> 10 July 1998

G.,E. *Arte contemporaneo y de calidad, Dos muestras de Judi Werthein* <u>El Cronista</u> 5 July 2000

Feinsilber ,Laura, *Tres Muy Buenas Exposiciones* <u>Ambito Financiero</u> 9 May 1996

Grinstein, Eva *Havana Biennal* <u>Flash Art</u> March-April, 2001 No. 217

Helguera, Pablo *Six feet under* <u>Art Nexus</u> February-April, 2001 No. 3

Israel, Nico *VII Bienal de La Habana* <u>Artforum</u> February 2001 p. 147-148

Katzenstein, Ines *The Work and the Gallery* Centro Cultural San Martin, Buenos Aires (catalogue) 2000

Kittelman, Udo *Jahresgaben 1998* Kolnischer Kunstverein, Cologne, Germany (catalogue)

Lawton, Pamela *Six feet under* <u>The New York Times</u> 7 August 2000

Lebenglik, Fabian *Judi Werthein Pelea con las Sombras* <u>Pagina 12</u> 21 May 1996

Lempka, Wayne *The Art of Memory* <u>Art New England</u> June/July 1998

Levin, Kim *Cuba Libre* <u>The Village Voice</u> 20 December 2000

Moynihan, Danny and Petruchansky, Hugo *Installation* Museum of Contemporary Art, Bahia Blanca, Argentina (catalogue) June 2000

Noorthoorn, Victoria <u>Judi Werthein</u> Galeria de Arte Ruth Benzacar, Buenos Aires (catalogue) June 2000

Noorthoorn, Victoria <u>Warning: Perception Requires Involvement</u> White Box Gallery, New York 2000

Noorthoorn, Victoria <u>The Challenge of Memory</u> Center for Curatorial Studies, Bard College, Annandale-on-Hudson, NY (catalogue) 1998

Verlichak, Victoria *A travez del tiempo* <u>Revistas Noticias</u> 1 July 1998

Zita, Carmen <u>*Judi Werthein: Paintings*</u> General Consulate of Argentina, New York, NY (catalogue) September 1997

Nov. 23/200 diciembre

Inventario de bienes que poseo:
Discurso tropical a mi medida
Ciudad arcano amor en la que leo
Suerte salud alcohol y despedida

Transfusiones de luz contra el mareo
El As de corazón, la fé perdida
Jamás creerme todo lo que veo
Volver al mar curar dolor herida

No pretendo cantar mi son entero
mirando tu perfil en la ventana
ni fabricar con mañas de embustero.

Sonetos de papel y porcelana
No intento seducirte, sólo quiero
Regalarte la nieve de
        la Habana,

Inventory of goods in my possession:
A tropical discourse made just for me
City secret love in which I read
Fortune health spirits and adieu

Transfusions of light to cure dizziness
The Ace of hearts, the faith I lost
Never believe in all the things I see
Return to sea to cure pain wound.

I don't intend to sing my full song
looking at your profile in the window
or to make up with a liar's tricks

my sonnets of paper and fine china.
I don't mean to seduce you, I just wish
to present you with the snow of Havana.

All photography taken in Havana, Cuba in November 2000

by Leandro Erlich y Judi Werthein
on the occasion of VII Bienal de La Habana

Special thanks to:
Barbara Hitchcock
Melissa Maldonado
Margarita Sanchez
Nelson Herrera Ysla
Hilda Maria Rodriguez
Ibis Fernandez Abascal
Yanet
Sra.Pampa Risso Patron
Cancilleria Argentina
Sra. Teresa Anchorena
Douglas Walla
POLAROID Foundation
Jorge Macchi
Zoel Daschuta
Hugo, Silvia and Mariano Sigman
Lito and Perla Erlich
Leo and Norma Werthein

Special materials funding for the project provided by
POLAROID

Book Design by
Tasha Sakhrani

Photographic ReMastering
Judi Werthein

Typeset in Futura
Produced by Uwe Kraus
Printed in Italy by Musumeci

First printing:
Hardcover Edition: 1000 copies

ISBN: 1-878607-99-5